This book has moth sketches that need to be colorized.

It's for kids and everyone who likes moths.

Just let your imagination free!

Created by Chris Taklis - March 2021

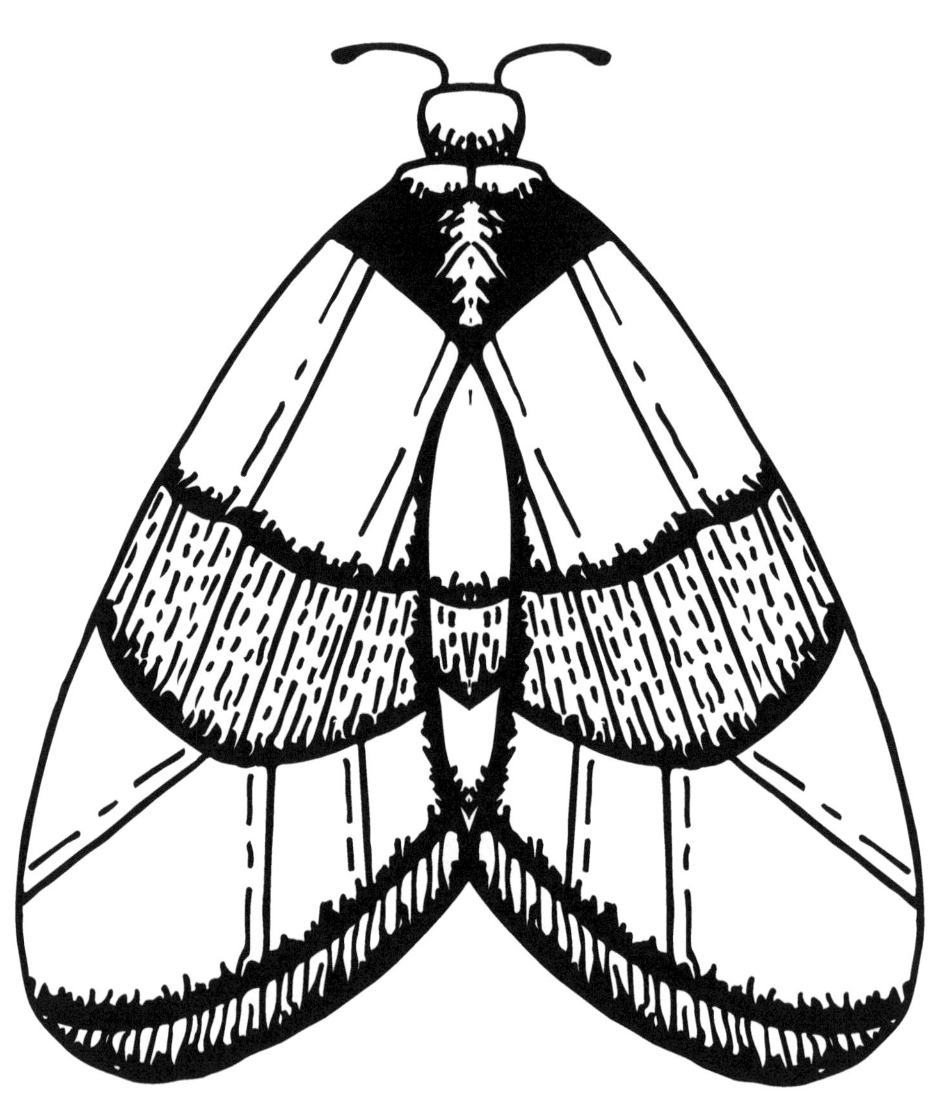

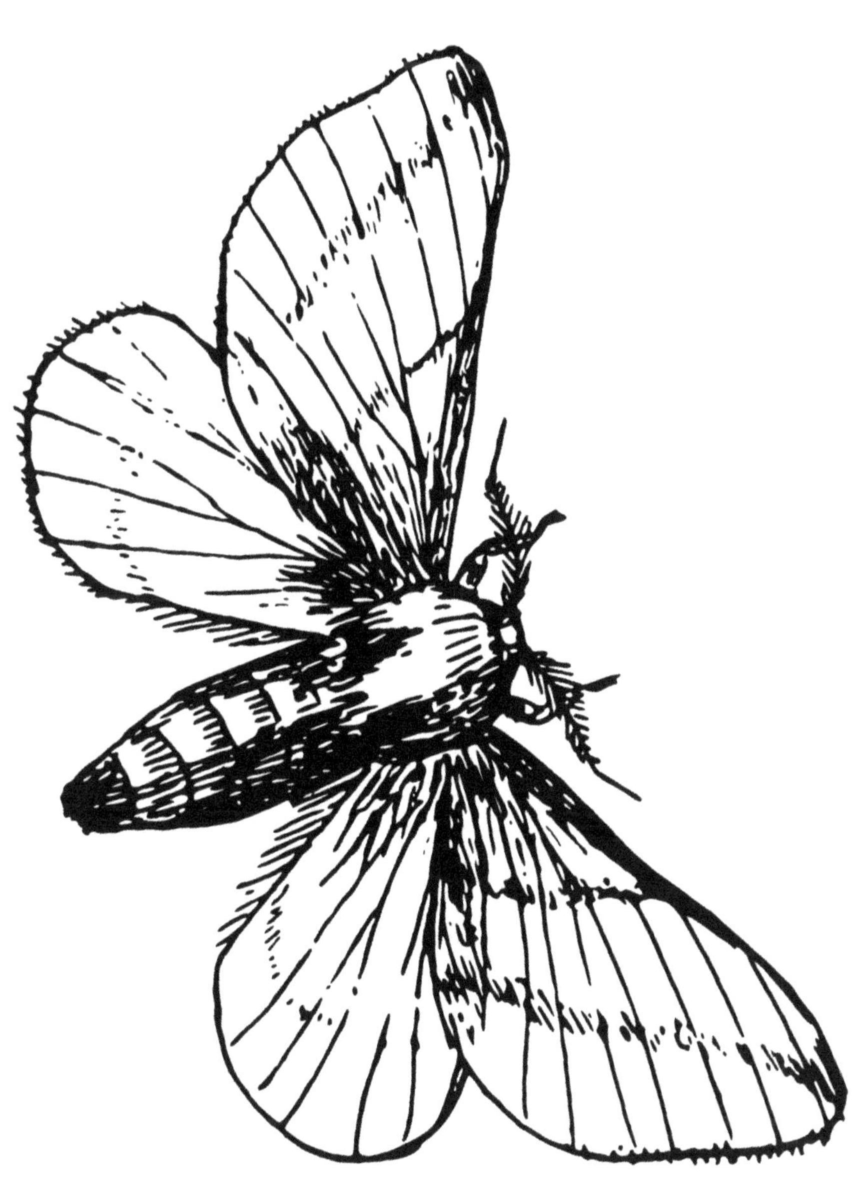

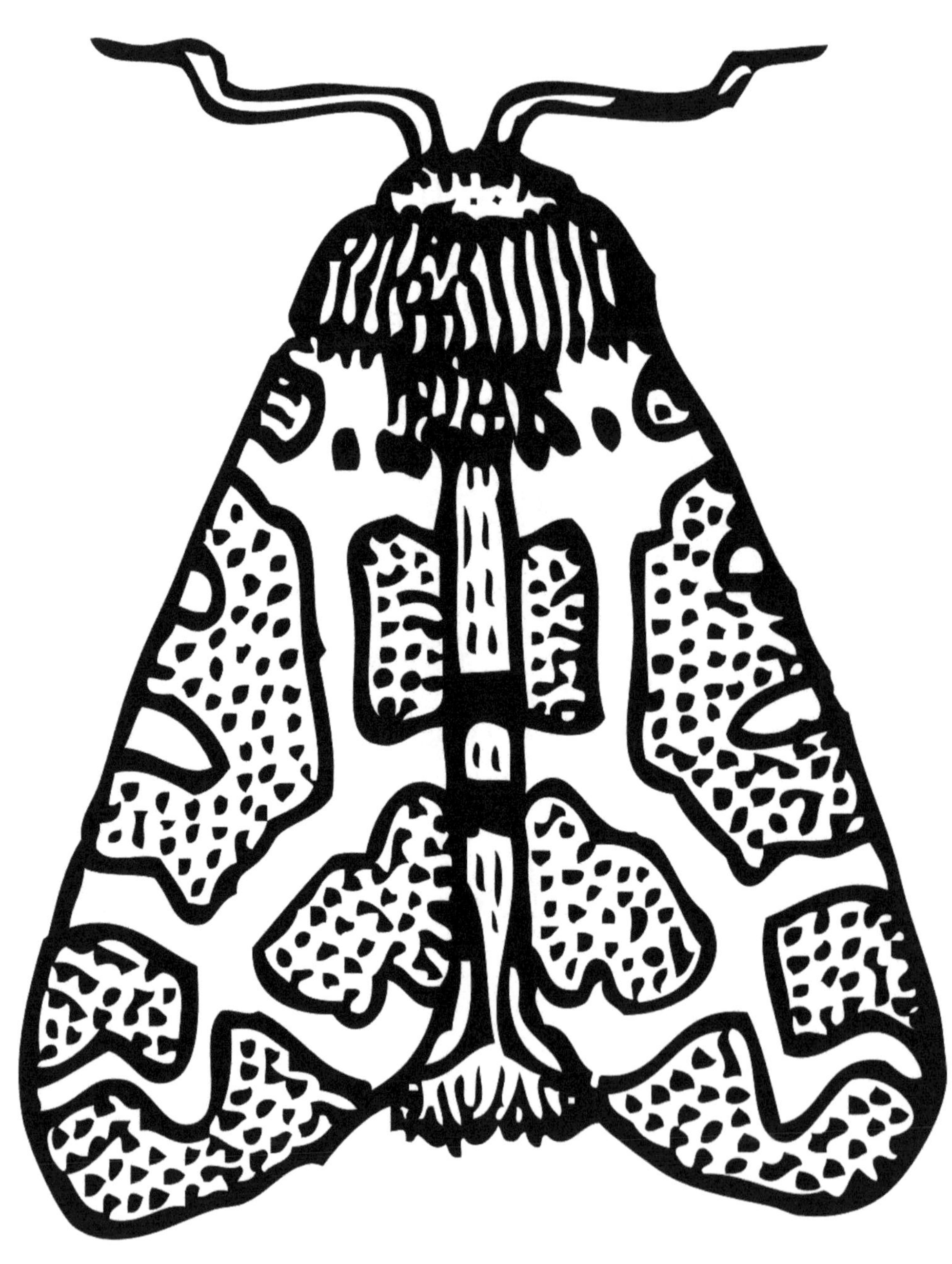

www.ingramcontent.com/pod-product-compliance
Ingram Content Group UK Ltd.
Pitfield, Milton Keynes, MK11 3LW, UK
UKHW022008190726
13853UKWH00004B/1802

9 798717 778558